words
i never
got spoken

how i remember
juvenile hall

Ali Moseley

Copyright © 2020 by Ali Moseley

Book Cover design by Lindsay Heider Diamond

All rights reserved. Printed in the United States of America. No part of this book may be used or reproduced in any manner whatsoever without written permission except in the case of brief quotations em-bodied in critical articles or reviews.

For information contact Authors Inside
P.O. Box 293, Oceano, CA 93475
WWW.AUTHORSINSIDE.ORG

ISBN: 978-1-954736-08-5
First Edition : February, 2021

words i never got spoken

how i remember juvenile hall

Ali Moseley

Also by Ali Moseley

Broken Wing (A Novel)

Heal My Broken Wing (self-help book)

Broken Wing : The Returning (A play)

Dedication,

for Luna and Breezy

Acknowledgements

Praise be to Allah Ta 'ala, the Merciful, the Compassionate, the Lord of the Two Worlds, and the blessings and peace be upon the Prince of the Prophets, our leader and master Muhammad ibn Abdullah; and his noble Companions and Family, whom Allah Ta 'ala bless and preserve with abiding and continuing peace and faith until the Day of Reckoning.

Much love to Margaret "Granny" Nicholson, Deloris Adams, and all my great uncles and aunts. My mom Sandra, my pop Big Larry, my daughter Breezy, and my bro and sis Josh and Sonja. Ellis and Denise, Celeste, Zeek, AJ, and Christina, Carla, and McKinley. My aunts, uncles, and cousins near and far. My extended family Miesha Byrd and Tootie Boss and fam. Dove. S.G. & M.J.K. Last but not least, my friends Anthony Sanchez and Reigh C. Ellis.

My friend and big sister Susan A. Phillips. My typist and bro Keith, the Dreaded Poet. Kanons. My business partner Chyna M. Sallier, the Lady Boss. The readers and writers of the Beat Within, who inspired me to push out this chapbook…Thank you. And my writing coach David Ochs…enjoy the journey.

Xtra special thanks to Emmanuel and Laura Gaisie, Lindsay Heider Diamond, Purple Pearls Publishing and Authors Inside.

"If someone calls it poetry, it's poetry."

-Ali Moseley

"Consider" (con sidere) means "with the stars" ; reconsider, means to rejoin the movement of heaven and life.

-Paul Hawken

Narrative poetry - which simply means "Story poems" - are among the oldest forms of literature. Like a novel or short story, a narrative poem has plot, characters, and setting. Narrative poems do not need rhyme. Before there were printed books, people would tell stories through narrative poems using rhythm, rhyme, repetition, and vivid language to make their tales easy to remember and share.

CONTENTS

HOW I REMEMBER JUVENILE HALL 1

TEN AWKWARD MINUTES 4

A HISTORY OF VIOLENCE 5

A NOTE 11

WHOOO BANGIN 16

CALABASAS NIGHT 18

ABOUT THE AUTHOR 28

HOW I REMEMBER JUVENILE HALL

I'm 14 years old
busted after a botched armed robbery
A gaggle of Sheriff and
Highway Patrol cars followed
our getaway car 2 miles
on the 10 Freeway. The police
helicopter cast a spotlight
over the rust-red Cadillac
wide enough to foil any
quick escape. I was
the sole juvenile.
I went to juvie, three others
to the county jail and the automobile
to the city impound.

I was 5'5', 135 pounds,
AND HELL ON WHEELS.
Wherever I found myself locked
behind wood, glass, or metal
I'd mule-kick the door till

words i never got spoken

someone peeked inside.
The face in the window
always threatened me with
loss of privileges and even
to come inside and kick
my scrawny little ass.
That worked on me to
back off the door.
Then, I'd put on a rap
concert rehashing every
rap song I'd ever heard!
Then I'd jerk-off in between
my bed sheets before lolling
off to sleep in the
middle of the day.

At night
I battled a piercing silence
for sleep that did not come and
visit me much in a room
with four walls and a slit
for a window. The one light

up on the celling cast a weak

arc on the walls, enough for

my hand puppet show, but

not much more.

And that's how I remember

the Hall.

TEN AWKWARD MINUTES

I went to trial on armed robbery./I put my hand on the Bible/and swore to tell the truth,/so help me God./I took the stand/and told lies so bold/nobody in the courtroom believed me,/including the Judge./Outcome: 3 years summary probation./When I got home,/my mother didn't believe/or want to hear me/about the creepy White guard who eye-balled me/for ten awkward minutes of silence/in a shower.

A HISTORY OF VIOLENCE (T.H.U.G.)

I'm 16 years old in the Hall
on trial for armed robbery
and 2nd degree attempted murder.
I had two co-D's, both gang members
like me. The three of us ripped the Hall
like pint-sized sticks of dynamite.
                    KABOOM!

Fistfights and gang activity got
me and my homeboys separated.
I pit stopped in a Senior Boys unit.
The staff were bigger, meaner, and
more aggressive toward boys.
Orientation: 10 minutes of
this-and-that talk by staff
about programs, services, policies,
procedures, and regulations.
I ain't have' ta listen but, I was

cautioned to obey those in authority

or get my scrawny ass kicked, locked-down,
and personal property trashed.
That *or* got my attention because these
two Black mofo staff were muscled
jocks with their sleeves rolled up
and baseball caps turned to the
back for action. I was poised
for action too as the dayroom
flooded with boys for chow.

Each kid walked a painted
stripe on the floor with
both hands pressed in
"county diamond" formation
behind his back. I saw
the faces of dozens who'd
already made the Hall
our home. They stare
with piercing eyes, their faces
rugged and their stubble chin
and mustaches of different
shades, dressed in scrubs
and worn Karate style shoes.

Some boys slouched in picnic chairs,
cornrows and afros matted to their heads,
others with green tats on arms
and shaved heads.
The aroma of soy taco meat
and yellow corn shells
interrupted my thoughts of
fighting long enough to
consider my stomach.
I always got fidgety before
I rumble. Like a nervous twitch.

I had a history of violence
with this kid LC. My gang
wore red; his gang wore blue,
both handkerchiefs Made in China.
LC and me were mortal enemies
in the street and the Hall.
LC sailed into the dayroom
under a hot gust of wind of
his own and sat right in front
of me. I started fudging with
my hands and pants as the heat

words i never got spoken

rose from the soles of my feet
to my head. We traded disses.
Suddenly, we leapt to our feet
and locked like two angry rams.
Staff were on both of us
in a flash! I got scoop-slammed
to the concrete floor by a
grown man. I was drug out
of the dayroom by my legs.
In the hallway, one man
chicken-winged me
and dropped a knee in
my lower back. The other
man called me all kinds
assholes and niggers as he
Matrix-punched on my head.
I could hear LC beg for mercy
somewhere behind me.
The Officer of the Day must have been
twisting LC because he was the
only other staff in the unit.
My body contorted; then,

I lay still. The shrieking
stopped, and all was silent.
It was over.

I'd taken my punishment
like a man and earned an
over-nighter in this jacked up
unit. My puffy eyes had
to adjust to the dingy
fluorescent light in my room.
The bunk was only 2-feet
wide and 6-feet long, a
couple of feet above the floor.
That night I found Claude Brown's
Man-child in the Promised Land.

I rolled over on my side,
the sharp pain in my
shoulder surging through my
chest. I sat up quickly,
momentarily bewildered. I
focused my thoughts. I opened
the book and with it
a window to the free world.

words i never got spoken

I began to read what I

could behind tears of rage
and mistrust for adults in
this prison society for children.

I hated these uppity-nigger
staff who'd twisted my wiry
frame into a pretzel for
laughs. The hate U gave
I give back to mothers
when I kill. That is the
cost of violence against
               children.

A NOTE

I met Goofy in the Gym.
The Gym used to be for
basketball, now it's a
transportation hub for
kids going north,
south, east, and west
in the Hall, everywhichaway
but home it seemed.

Goofy was looking wet
with her slick black hair
rolled into a bagel bun,
her acne-free skin set to
the tone of butter on toast.
She wore a white pullover
and yellow floppy pants
and black slip-ons.
She had tats.

There was a sea of kids
in custody. Staff was busy

words i never got spoken

dressing Thuggys in belly
chains and handcuffs and leg
irons like slaves for transport.
It was a wonder
that our eyes caught
across the Gym. I smiled.
She smiled.
I knew I had to somehow
get closer to this girl
if I wanted to make
her mine before I caught
the next line movement
to my unit.

I dipped into the restroom
came out and sat in the
row of benches across from
Goofy and her friends.
I had to play it off.
You know how staff
be blockin' girls
from boys in the Hall.
I asked her name. Goofy?
What kinda name's that
for a girl? She shrugged
her shoulders. She told

me that she tried to laugh
and have a fun time ev' day.
Her smile was electric!
Perfect white teeth with
small spaces between them
and bright eyes. Wow.
I asked her to write me
a note sometime and
shoot it through staff.
She promised she would.
I caught the next line
movement to my unit.
I looked back once,
twice, just before the
Gym exit and Goofy
was already talking to
another ninja. She prolly
promised to write him
a note too. *Humf!*

I was feelin' some kinda
way when a week passed
and my note never touchdown.
Maybe staff was hating.
Maybe Goofy forgot my unit.
Maybe she was busy writing
ninjas in other units. I was

words i never got spoken

about to snap. No. I'd
straighten things out with
"My Girl" at church on Sunday.

A note meant a lot. I didn't
get mail from home. Never
got visits. Hardly even used
the brown phone after my
"G" on the street drop-kicked
Ya Boy in the chest. Forreal.

I practically begged my parents
to let this girl stay at my crib
after her mom kicked
her out and she had no place
to go for 2 days. I was in
the Hall 2 months and
she was already slidin'
with another ninja.
Can you believe that?
Anyway, I creased my
pants with soap and a
fine-tooth unbreakable
comb and left the flops
under my mat to iron out
the wrinkles.

Sunday church.
I low-key threw up
the set to the homies
and suckas alike in
a jam packed chapel.
The girls sat in the first
two rows in front of the
stage. There was no way
for me to reach Goofy
from row 15. My hopes
were dashed. Then a group
of girls took the stage.
There was Goofy
                    my girl
reading a Bible verse.
               My G.
I had to wonder
how many other fellas
was thinking what I
was thinking in the chapel.
I didn't get to talk to Goofy
that day but we did
catch eyes for the longest,

sweetest 2 and a half
seconds of my life as

words i never got spoken

the girls went out the
Exit. I never did get
a note from Goofy.

WHOOO BANGIN

My roommate Chewy and me
were kicking back in our
room in the Hall. A disturbance
started down the hallway in
another room. Something about
taking a wiz. There are no toilets
inside the rooms. The boys in room 9
were bamming on the door. Staff
followed the noise to 9. He told
these two to "knock it off," headcalls
and dayroom would begin in an hour
or so. The boys in 9 said something
staff didn't like. Suddenly, he
unclipped a family-sized OC spray
can on his hip. He gave the can
a good shake. He warned these two knuckleheads
to stay off the door.
Someone inside 9 mule-kicked the
door. Staff unlocked the door,
super-soaked the room, locked it again.
Staff disappeared down the hallway
to his office.
The OC gas leaked from
9 into the hallway. We were blinded,
shielding our eyes. We stuffed
blankets and sheets in door

words i never got spoken

jams and cracks to keep
the tear gas out. A fire started
in my belly and crawled up my chest.
The room had windows that didn't open
one way or another. We were all locked
in. Chewy told me to wrap my towel
over my face, he'd seen it in the movies.
Somebody in the hallway started a
"Whooo Bang!" Every kid
on the hallway mule-kicked the
doors with everything we had
shouting, "Whooo Bang!" in chorus.
Whooo Bang mofo!
Make enough noise and staff
will respond. *Whooo Bang! Mofo!*
Staff opened the unit exits.
A thin mist like a vapor rolled over
the room doors and seemed to turn
corners as if it were looking for
something in the unit.

There was a sinister essence about this staff/walking the unit perimeter. /Something unnatural about his cold dead eyes/peeking in my window. /I glanced past his shoulder/and saw a glimpse of the sun moving higher/on the horizon in my window looking in on the Hall.

words i never got spoken

CALABASAS NIGHT

The van drove 2-hours across
Los Angeles freeways to the
Boondocks. I ain't try to
trace our route by looking
out becuz the honeycomb
screen on the windows only
add to my motion sickness.
Besides, I really ain't care
where I was going. I burned
inside with the time I had
at camp community placement.
1-year minimum at Senior Boys
probation camp.

"Here we are boys,"
said the black man who called
himself Coach. " Calabasas."
The van took a road by a hill,
a field ugly and grass covered.
It was a leveled expanse of
ground perhaps 2-acres
enveloped by rolling hills.
Around the campground a
15 -foot tall redbrick wall.
                       Camp Gonzales?

It had to be way out here

in the middle of nowhere.
I had no idea where Calabasas is.
Coach made a sharp right turn
and the van bounced as it

rolled over a primitive car path
on the rough ground. Through
the windshield I saw the glare of
sunlight bounce off cars parked on
the way. Coach bumped the automobile
horn and a wall of metal lumbered open
for the van. The van pulled inside and
the gate closed behind.
Tick-tock, tick-tock.
I sat stiffly in the backseat; my T-shirt
damp with sweat and sticking to my body.
My eyes squinting slightly, betraying
the fact that the fear was not negligible.
I knew the ropes. I knew the dangers.

Camp Gonzo is Gladiator School
for 16, 17, and 18 year olds.
I fought. I made weapons.
I forged county documents.
I participated in gang rumbles.
I smoked contraband cigs.
I ditched school. I robbed other kids.
I stole food from the chow hall.
I manipulated the telephone and mail systems.
I was always into something and my PO
was always on my case about it.

*I remember a time at Camp Gonzo
with Mr. H.*

*The red-orange sun burned
a hole in the streaked blue tapestry
that was the evening sky. Areas of
yellow rimmed the lower clouds; a
purplish -black void was above.
A soft Calabasas night would soon
envelop this section of LA County.
It would be dark when the camp
exercise yard opened. Mr. H and me
sat at a picnic table and stared out at
the horizon over tint ed grass of canyon
hills. Staff was in side the control
bubble behind us, sleep. ZZZZZ.*

*Mr. H had the best manners,
slightly aloof and very proper
with just the right traces of
unfelt humility.
I don't remember anything
he said to me this night
but I'll never forget
how he made me feel
my 17th birthday.*
   Ordinarily human.

And with the famous words of James Joyce: /"The Heaventree of stars hung with humid night bluc Fruit." /A Calabasas night.

words i never got spoken

Ali's Corner

In 2007, I was sentenced to life with the possibility of parole. I was twenty-eight years old. I wrote books with restorative justice themes and spoke to the fellow prisoners about making the right choices and decisions. That led to founding my own company City of Angelz publishing.

At every self-help group and prison that I entered, I told my personal story of redemption. Although I felt I did a great deal to redeem myself personally, I also knew that I had an obligation to do my part toward stemming the tide of hopelessness and criminality that had plagued my generation for so long. Because of the influence my generation had on America's youth by escalating the gang epidemic, I knew I still had a very steep debt to pay off.

Now, I invite you to take our #DontShootPledge.

I, _____ , promise to never carry or fire live ammunition on or around schools, churches, playgrounds, or public malls in America.

Now talk about it, tell a friend you took the pledge! Post it. Tweet it. #DontShootPledge

Sincerely,

Ali

An Interview with Ali Moseley by Ray Czar

Q: What is most important to you in life?

A: Most important to me is maintaining my relationship with God as I understand Him. Through that very special relationship I honor the memory of Tre, my family, my friends, and myself. Recognizing that God is always present shines light on my world and now I see people, places, and things as they really are and not how I imagine them to be.

Q: How do you find/make friends?

A: I have a built-in "friend detector" that allows me to come closer to good people and back off bad people. Generally, look for friends with good vibes, good hygiene, and common sense. Friendship is organic - it grows out of nothing, like a plant in the soil. So, make sure the soil is right. I also recognize that most friends are really only for a season, meaning, people move on in life and close friends can become long distance friends. Only a handful of friendships last for a lifetime.

Q: Where does education rate 1-10?

A: Education is a 10! Knowledge is a game changer. Go to school. Get good grades. Graduate.

Q: What's your greatest fear?

A: I fear going to Hell and roasting like a plucked chicken on the Devil's pitchfork.

Q: Do you have a hero?

A: My Mom is my hero. I took my Mom through a lot. She had my back through seven court trials. She always made me go to school. She helped raise my daughter. She traveled long trips to visit me in prison. She sent me money and care packages for 20 years in prison. She taught me the definition of unconditional love. Shout out to MOM! Now I make Mom proud by living my best life. That's all she ever wanted for me.

An Excerpt from W.I.N.G.S. Vol. II

Hardest Person To Please

The person I find hardest to please is Tre. I guess it's hard to please him becuz I made some awfully hard promises to keep with him. I used to gangbang. I left the gang 10 years ago and promised Tre I'd never go back to my gang fam or that ratchet lifestyle.

But everywhere I go in prison I run into homies from the set. They always want to know what's up with me. I tell 'em I'ma man and I got a promise to keep to someone special.

I promised Tre I was done with smoking weed and drinking liquor. Some days I just wanna get my mind right and xscape the boredom of prison, but I just say No when dudes invite me to wake 'n' bake. I gave Tre my word I'd never pickup another illegal cellphone in prison. When I see a cellphone I lower my eyes and keep it movin'.
                        straight up!
I swore to Tre I'd never forget June 24th, 2004. That's the day we first met.

Tre been by my side since 1p.m., Wednesday, summer 04.

So, whenever I'm tempted to break a promise I remind myself that I gotta do it someplace where Tre won't see me; but that's impossible becuz eventho I don't see Tre I know he sees me.
                        He's a spirit.

And even though Tre was involved in gangs like I was it don't mean I had the right to take his life. And for that reason
I owe Tre
the rest of my life.
I love you bro.

Rest in Peace

About the Author

Ali was born in Los Angeles, California, in April 1979, the son of Larry ("Red"), an emergency medical technician (EMT), and his then-wife Sandra, a police radio dispatcher. Ali grew up in the Pueblo del Rio housing project before living in the Florence area, followed by a tough neighborhood in Altadena, CA. He is the oldest of one brother, one sister, and two cousins who all grew up under the same roof. At age 13, he joined the notorious Pueblo Bishop Bloods. During a rough-and-tumble childhood and on a mission to make a name for himself with his homies, he often found himself incarcerated in places such as Central, Los Padrinos, and Sylmar juvenile hall, Challenger, and Camp Gonzales.

In 2007, he was convicted of first-degree murder, attempted murder, and sentenced to four consecutive life sentences in state prison. This experience affected him profoundly. At age 28, Ali decided that he had enough of living on the edge and took the "shahadda" and entered the fold of Al-Islam.

Ali will not surrender his dreams. He has launched his own publishing company and gone on to write many other short stories, screenplays, plays, and music that he hopes will touch the hearts and minds of people everywhere. God Willing.

Other books by AUTHORS INSIDE

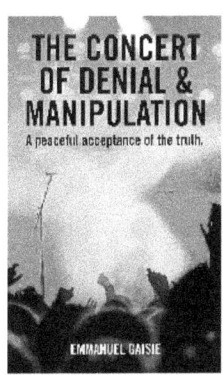

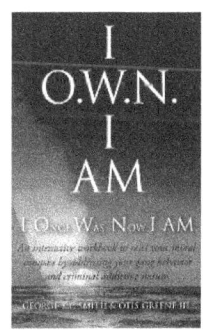

www.ingramcontent.com/pod-product-compliance
Lightning Source LLC
Chambersburg PA
CBHW071231160426
43196CB00012B/2484